More of Janice VanCleave's Wild, Wacky, and Weird ASTRONOMY EXPERIMENTS

Illustrations by
Lorna William

ROSEN
PUBLISHING

NEW YORK

This edition published in 2017 by
The Rosen Publishing Group, Inc.
29 East 21st Street
New York, NY 10010

Library of Congress Cataloging-in-Publication Data

Names: VanCleave, Janice.
Title: More of Janice VanCleave's wild, wacky, and weird astronomy experiments / Janice VanCleave.
Description: New York : Rosen YA, 2017. | Series: Janice Vancleave's wild, wacky, and weird science experiments | Includes index.
Identifiers: LCCN ISBN 9781499465372 (pbk.) | ISBN 9781499465396 (library bound) | ISBN 9781499465389 (6-pack)
Subjects: LCSH: Astronomy—Experiments—Juvenile literature.
Classification: LCC QB46.V364 2016 | DDC 520.78—dc23

Manufactured in the United States of America

Illustrations by Lorna William

Experiments first published in *Janice VanCleave's 202 Oozing, Bubbling, Dripping, and Bouncing Experiments* by John Wiley & Sons, Inc. copyright © 1996 Janice VanCleave and *Janice VanCleave's 200 Gooey, Slippery, Slimy, Weird and Fun Experiments* by John Wiley & Sons, Inc. copyright © 1992 Janice VanCleave

CONTENTS

INTRODUCTION

Since the beginning of humankind, people have looked to the heavens to try to understand the stars, the planets, and our sun. In modern times, we have rocketed into space to land on the moon. We have built an International Space Station to do research in space and powerful telescopes to peer at the far reaches of the universe. Perhaps humans will someday visit Mars.

Astronomy is the study of the planets, the stars, and other bodies in space. The people who decide to work in the field of astronomy have a variety of career paths to choose from. Some scientists study the planets and others study galaxies. Some astronomers work to learn more about black holes and the universe. Solar scientists focus on our sun, the star that enables life to exist on Earth. All of these people have something in common: They are constantly asking questions to learn even more about space.

This book is a collection of science experiments about astronomy. Why are astronauts taller in space? Why do Jupiter's rings shine? When is Mercury most visible from Earth? You will find the answers to these and many other questions by doing the experiments in this book.

HOW TO USE THIS BOOK

You will be rewarded with successful experiments if you read each experiment carefully, follow the steps in order, and do not substitute materials. The following sections are included for all the experiments.

4

» **PURPOSE:** *The basic goals for the experiment.*

» **MATERIALS:** *A list of supplies you will need.* You will experience less frustration and more fun if you gather all the necessary materials for the experiments before you begin. You lose your train of thought when you have to stop and search for supplies.

» **PROCEDURE:** *Step-by-step instructions on how to perform the experiment.* Follow each step very carefully, never skip steps, and do not add your own. Safety is of the utmost importance, and by reading the experiment before starting, then following the instructions exactly, you can feel confident that no unexpected results will occur. Ask an adult to help you when you are working with anything sharp or hot. If adult supervision is required, it will be noted in the experiment.

» **RESULTS:** *An explanation stating exactly what is expected to happen.* This is an immediate learning tool. If the expected results are achieved, you will know that you did the experiment correctly. If your results are not the same as described in the experiment, carefully read the instructions and start over from the first step.

» **WHY?** *An explanation of why the results were achieved.*

INTRODUCTION

THE SCIENTIFIC METHOD

Scientists identify a problem or observe an event. Then they seek solutions or explanations through research and experimentation. By doing the experiments in this book, you will learn to follow experimental steps and make observations. You will also learn many scientific principles that have to do with astronomy.

In the process, the things you see or learn may lead you to new questions. For example, perhaps you have completed the experiment that uses a mirror to demonstrate how radio waves are sent around Earth via satellite. Now you wonder what would happen if you changed the angle of the mirror. That's great! All scientists are curious and ask new questions about what they learn. When you design a new experiment, it is a good idea to follow the scientific method.

1. Ask a question.

2. Do some research about your question. What do you already know?

3. Come up with a hypothesis, or a possible answer to your question.

4. Design an experiment to test your hypothesis. Make sure the experiment is repeatable.

5. Collect the data and make observations.

6. Analyze your results.

7. Reach a conclusion. Did your results support your hypothesis?

Many times the experiment leads to more questions and a new experiment.

Always remember that when devising your own science experiment, have a knowledgeable adult review it with you before trying it out. Ask them to supervise it as well.

FOCUS

PURPOSE To determine why radio wave receivers are curved.

MATERIALS scissors
index card
modeling clay
sheet of black construction paper
6-by-12-inch (15-by-30-cm) piece of aluminum foil
quart (liter) jar
flashlight

PROCEDURE

1. Cut four 1-inch (2.5-cm)- high slits in the index card, about 1/4 inch (0.6 cm) wide and 1/4 inch (0.6 cm) apart.

2. Use clay to stand the card in the center of the paper.

3. Fold the aluminum foil in half lengthwise three times.

4. Mold the aluminum foil around the side of the jar to form a curved metal mirror.

5. Place the flashlight on one side of the card and the curved aluminum mirror on the opposite side.

6. In a darkened room, move the flashlight toward and away from the card until straight lines of light pass through the slits in the card.

7. Move the aluminum toward and away from the card until the clearest image is seen.

RESULTS Lines of light reflected from the aluminum mirror leave the surface of the metal at an angle and cross at one point in front of the mirror.

WHY? Light is reflected from the concave (crescent shaped) mirror to a central focal point. Radio waves, like the light, can be reflected from concave surfaces to a point where a type of microphone is positioned to send the concentrated waves on to another receiver.

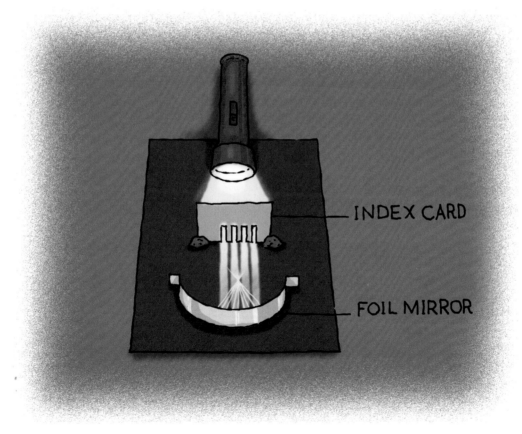

INDEX CARD

FOIL MIRROR

AROUND THE WORLD

PURPOSE To demonstrate how radio waves are sent around the earth via satellite.

MATERIALS small coffee can
black construction paper
transparent tape
yardstick (meter stick)
scissors
modeling clay
flat mirror
flashlight

PROCEDURE

1. Cover the outside of the can with the paper.

2. Tape a paper flap about 4 inches (10 cm) square to one side of the can.

3. Place the measuring stick in front of the can.

4. Use the clay to stand the mirror on top of the measuring stick near the can.

5. Darken the room. Place the flashlight at a slight angle to the can as shown.

6. Move the mirror and flashlight until light from the flashlight is projected onto the paper flap.

RESULTS The mirror changes the direction of the light path.

WHY? In this experiment the mirror represents a satellite above Earth (the can). Light from the flashlight represents radio waves and the paper is a receiver. The direction of the light is changed by reflecting it off a mirror. The direction of radio waves can also be changed by sending them to a satellite that sends them in another direction.

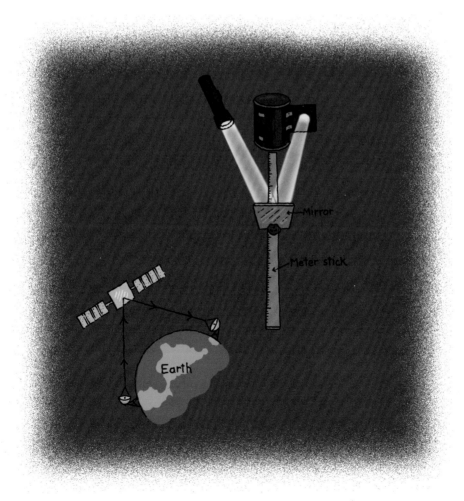

LAUNCHER

PURPOSE To demonstrate how satellites are launched into orbit around Earth.

MATERIALS cardboard box
2 plastic rulers with grooves down the center
modeling clay
marble

PROCEDURE

1. Place the cardboard box upside down on a table, with the edge of the box 10 inches (25 cm) from the edge of the table.

2. Lay one ruler on top of the box with 4 inches (10 cm) of the ruler extending over the edge of the box. This ruler will be called the launcher.

3. Hold the other ruler so that one end touches the launcher, with their grooves lined up, and the second end is supported with clay 2 inches (5 cm) above the box. The raised ruler represents power rockets.

4. Position a marble at the top of the raised ruler, and then release the marble. The marble represents a satellite.

RESULTS The marble rolls down the rulers and off the end. Its path curves until it hits the floor.

WHY? The table represents Earth. The top of the box is a position above Earth's surface. All satellites are raised to the desired height above Earth by booster rockets and then turned, so that with additional power rockets, the satellite is launched parallel to Earth's surface. The marble satellite, like space satellites, moves in a curved path because gravity pulls it down as its launching speed pushes it forward.

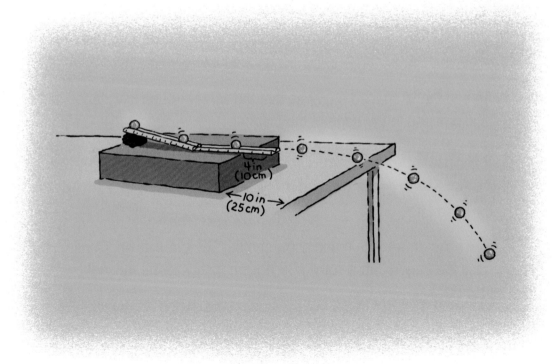

ESCAPE

PURPOSE To demonstrate escape velocity.

MATERIALS 12-by-4-inch (30-by-10-cm) strip of stiff paper
magnet, any size or shape
large plastic lid
transparent tape
modeling clay
box of steel air-gun shot, BBs

PROCEDURE

1. Fold the paper lengthwise to form an M shape.

2. Place the magnet against the inside edge of the plastic lid.

3. Spread the M-shaped paper so that the center trough is widened, and tape one end to the edge of the magnet.

4. Use the clay to slightly elevate the unattached end of the paper trough.

5. Place one BB at the top of the trough and allow it to roll toward the magnet.

6. Raise the trough again and allow another BB to roll down. Continue to raise the trough until a rolling BB does not stick to the magnet.

RESULTS The BBs roll down the trough and stick to the magnet when the trough is slightly raised. At a higher elevation, the BBs slow down when they touch the magnet, but roll past into the plastic lid.

WHY? Raising the trough increases the velocity, or speed, of the BBs.

14

The velocity of the BBs can be compared to the escape velocity (velocity needed to escape Earth's gravitational pull) of a rocket leaving Earth. The BBs are escaping the magnetic pull of the magnet, and the rocket is escaping the gravitational pull of the planet.

BLAST OFF

PURPOSE To demonstrate how rockets move in space.

MATERIALS 9-inch (23-cm) balloon

PROCEDURE

1. Inflate the balloon and hold the mouth of the balloon shut between your fingers.

2. Release the balloon and allow it to move freely.

RESULTS The balloon moves around the room as it deflates.

WHY? When the inflated balloon is closed, the air inside pushes equally in all directions. As the air leaves the balloon, the opening moves back and forth, like a rudder, which directs the balloon in an irregular path through the air. The balloon, like a rocket, moves because of Newton's Third Law of Motion, which states that for every action there is an equal and opposite reaction. In the case of the balloon, the rubber pushes on the air inside (action), forcing it out the opening. The air pushes on the balloon (reaction). The reaction force of the air pushes the balloon in the opposite direction of the action force. Like the balloon, spacecraft are able to move forward due to action-reaction forces. The engines of a rocket produce gases that are pushed out the exhaust (action), and the gas applies a force on the rocket (reaction). The reaction force pushes against the rocket, causing it to lift up.

REACTION FORCE

ACTION FORCE

REACTION
FORCE

ACTION
FORCE

POINTER

PURPOSE To demonstrate how a gyroscope helps steer a spacecraft.

MATERIALS large plastic lid from a can, such as a coffee can
18-inch (45-cm) piece of string
modeling clay
round toothpick
full-length mirror
adult helper

PROCEDURE

1. Ask an adult to make a hole in the center of the plastic lid.

2. Thread the free end of the string through the hole and tie a knot on the underside.

3. Press a grape-sized piece of clay in the center of the lid on top of the knot. Stand the toothpick in the center of the clay.

4. Stand in front of the mirror and hold the string. Use your hand to start the lid spinning. This action also starts the lid swinging back and forth.

5. While looking in the mirror, continue swinging the lid back and forth. Observe the direction the toothpick points.

RESULTS If the lid is spun fast enough, it spins horizontally, with the toothpick pointing straight down.

WHY? The lid acts like a gyroscope, an instrument with a wheel or disk designed to spin around a central axis. As long as the lid spins rapidly, the direction of its spin axis, the toothpick, will not change. The resistance of a gyroscope's spin axis to change in direction makes it a useful device for aiming and steering spacecraft.

SPHERES

PURPOSE To simulate the release of a drop of liquid in space.

MATERIALS clear drinking glass
eyedropper
tap water
liquid cooking oil
rubbing alcohol

PROCEDURE

CAUTION: Keep the alcohol away from your nose and mouth.

1. Fill the glass half full with water.

2. Tilt the glass and very slowly fill the glass with alcohol by pouring the alcohol down the inside of the glass. This will keep it from mixing with the water.

3. Add 4 to 5 drops of oil to the glass.

4. Observe the position of the oil and its shape.

RESULTS The oil falls through the alcohol and spheres of oil float between the alcohol and water layer.

WHY? The oil drops stay suspended between the layers of water and alcohol because the oil does not dissolve in either liquid. The oil is heavier than the alcohol but lighter than the water, and thus it falls through the alcohol and floats on the surface of the water. This produces the same results as releasing a drop of liquid in space. In both situations, the liquid drop forms a near perfect sphere (ball shape).

OIL →

Cooking
Oil

RUBBING
ALCOHOL

ALCOHOL

WATER

PROTECTOR

PURPOSE To determine how the materials in space suits help to regulate temperature.

MATERIALS 2 drinking glasses
rubber glove
aluminum foil
cotton handkerchief
2 thermometers
desk lamp

PROCEDURE

1. Line one glass with the rubber glove, and cover the outside of the glass with aluminum foil.

2. Line the other glass with the handkerchief.

3. Place a thermometer in each glass and set both glasses about 12 inches (30 cm) from the lamp.

4. Observe the temperature on both thermometers after 5 minutes.

RESULTS The temperature is higher in the glass lined with the handkerchief.

WHY? Insulators are materials that help prevent temperature changes by slowing the transfer of heat energy. The rubber glove is a better insulator than the handkerchief. The aluminum foil helps keep the glass cooler by reflecting light away from the glass. An astronaut's space suit must keep a constant temperature, and one way is to decrease the amount of heat transferred to and from the astronaut's body. Layers of insulating nylon materials are used to make the suits. When worn outside the spacecraft, an outer garment made of aluminized plastic and fireproofing material is worn over the suit. This adds thermal and micrometeroid protection. Insulated gloves and boots are also worn.

SPACE SUIT

PURPOSE To demonstrate how a space suit affects an astronaut's blood.

MATERIALS sealed bottle of soda
timer

PROCEDURE

1. Observe the liquid in the sealed bottle of soda for 10 to 15 seconds.

2. Open the bottle of soda.

3. Observe the liquid in the bottle for 10 to 15 seconds.

RESULTS No bubbles are seen in the sealed bottle, but gas bubbles rise to the surface of the liquid in the open bottle.

WHY? In the bottling process, high pressure is used to cause carbon dioxide gas to dissolve in the soda water. When the bottle is opened, the pressure decreases and a large amount of the gas rises to the surface of the liquid and escapes into the air. The pressure inside a space suit is great enough to keep dissolved gases in an astronaut's blood. If the space suit were punctured, the pressure inside the suit would decrease and bubbles of gas would come out of the blood as the bubbles in the soda did. Not only would gas bubbles escape the blood, but bubbles of gas inside the blood vessels could expand, causing the vessels to break.

Space Suit

FAKE

PURPOSE To demonstrate how artificial gravity can be produced.

MATERIALS scissors

sheet of construction paper, any color

round cake pan

turntable

4 marbles

PROCEDURE

1. Cut a circle of paper to fit inside the pan.

2. Center the pan on the turntable.

3. Place the marbles in the center of the pan.

4. Turn the turntable.

RESULTS As the pan starts to spin, the marbles move forward until they hit the side of the pan.

WHY? The movement of the pan starts the marbles moving. They move in a straight line until the side of the pan stops them. The marbles then press against the pan's side as long as the pan turns. In space, a turning space station would cause unattached objects inside to be pressed against the walls of the station just as the marbles press against the turning pan. A spinning space station would provide artificial gravity to allow astronauts to walk around. The artificial grvity would also let dropped objects fall "down," rather than floating, "down" being toward the outside rim of the turning craft. The most likely shape for a spinning space station would be a large wheel.

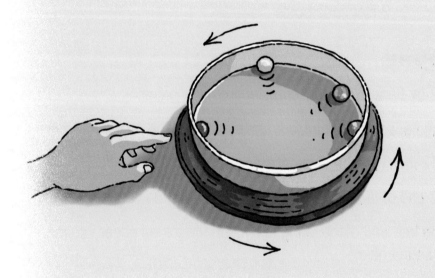

Fake

WEIGHTLESSNESS

PURPOSE To determine why astronauts orbiting Earth have a feeling of weightlessness.

MATERIALS scissors
ruler
sheet of construction paper, any color
transparent tape
string
2-liter soda bottle

PROCEDURE

1. Cut a 2-by-8-inch (5-by-20-cm) strip from the paper.

2. Fold the paper strip in half four times and tape the edges together.

3. Cut a 12-inch (30-cm) piece of string.

4. Tie one end of the string around the center of the folded paper.

5. Hold the free end of the string and insert the folded paper into the plastic soda bottle.

6. Pull up on the string until the bottle is about 2 inches (5 cm) above the table.

7. Release the string.

8. Observe the movement of the bottle and the folded paper.

RESULTS When the string is released, the bottle and the paper fall. The paper hangs at the top of the bottle until the bottle stops, and then the paper falls to the bottom of the bottle.

WHY? Like the paper and bottle, astronauts and the spacecraft they are in fall at the same speed while orbiting Earth. As long as both are falling there is an apparent weightlessness (zero pull of gravity).

TALLER

PURPOSE To determine how gravity affects height.

MATERIALS scissors
2-liter soda bottle with cap
5 empty plastic thread spools
18-inch (45-cm) length of string
2-quart (2-liter) bowl
large pitcher of tap water
adult helper

PROCEDURE

1. Ask an adult to remove the bottom from the soda bottle.

2. Place the string in the bottle with about 2 inches (5 cm) of string hanging out of the mouth of the bottle.

3. Secure the cap on the bottle, leaving part of the string hanging out.

4. Thread the free end of the string through the holes in the spools.

5. Set the bottle, cap side down, in the bowl.

6. Support the bottle in an upright position with your hand, and hold the upper end of the string with your free hand so that the spools stand straight. Notice the position of each spool.

7. Ask your helper to fill the plastic bottle with water while you continue to pull the string upward. Again, notice the position of each spool.

RESULTS In the bottle full of water, the spools are separated and the top spool is higher in the bottle.

WHY? The upward force by the water, called buoyancy, simulates a low-gravity environment. With less downward pull, the spools separate. Like the spools, the spine has a cord called the spinal cord (a large bundle of nerves that runs through the centers of the discs of the spine). Gravity pulls the discs down against each other. In space, the discs separate, and the spine gets longer because gravity is not pulling it down. Thus, astronauts are taller in space.

Taller

OVERHEAD

PURPOSE To find the zenith of an object.

MATERIALS 8-inch (20-cm) piece of string

12-inch (30-cm) ruler, with holes for a 3-ring binder

scissors

masking tape

pen

PROCEDURE

1. Tie one end of the string to the hole in one end of the ruler.

2. Stick a 1-inch (2.5-cm)-long piece of tape on the end of the ruler that has the string.

3. Draw an arrow on the tape so that the arrow points toward the string.

4. Hold the end of the string and raise your arm so that the ruler hangs in front of you.

5. Observe the direction the arrow points.

NOTE: Keep the ruler for the next experiment.

RESULTS The arrow points up.

WHY? Gravity pulls the hanging ruler toward the center of Earth. Thus, the bottom of the ruler points straight down and the top of the ruler points straight up. Imagine a line going straight up from the top of the ruler and ending at a point in the sky directly above the ruler. That point is called the zenith (point in the sky directly above that object) of the ruler. Your zenith is different from that of the ruler. No two objects can have the same zenith at the same time because no two objects occupy the same space at the same time.

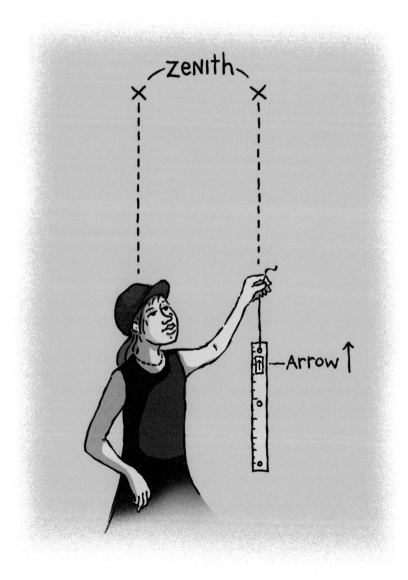

BELOW

PURPOSE To find the nadir of an object.

MATERIALS scissors
masking tape
pen
ruler from previous experiment

PROCEDURE

1. Cut a piece of tape about 1 inch (2.5 cm) long.

2. Stick the tape to the end of the ruler opposite the previously taped end.

3. Draw an arrow on the tape so that the two arrows on the ruler point in opposite directions.

4. Hold the end of the string and raise your arm so the ruler hangs in front of you.

5. Observe the direction of both arrows.

RESULTS One arrow points up and the other points down.

WHY? Gravity pulls the bottom of the ruler toward the center of Earth; thus, the bottom arrow points toward Earth's center. Imagine a line going from the bottom arrow through Earth to a point in the sky on the opposite side of the planet. That point is called the nadir of the ruler. The nadir of an object is the point in the sky directly below that object on the other side of Earth, opposite the object's zenith.

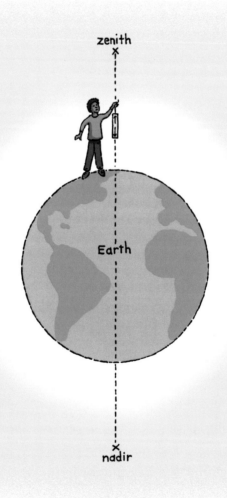

TOO CLOSE

PURPOSE To determine how distance from the sun affects atmospheric temperature.

MATERIALS 2 thermometers
1 desk lamp
yardstick (meter stick)

PROCEDURE

1. Place one thermometer on the 4 inches (10 cm) mark and the second thermometer on the 36 inches (100 cm) mark of the yardstick (meter stick).

2. Position the lamp close to the 0 end of the yardstick (meter stick).

3. Turn the lamp on.

4. Read and record the temperatures on both thermometers after 10 minutes.

RESULTS The temperature is hotter on the closer thermometer.

WHY? The thermometer closer to the lamp receives more energy and thus gets hotter. As the light moves away from the lamp, rays leaving at an angle do not hit the distant thermometer. The atmosphere of a planet is heated in a similar way. Mercury is the planet closest to the sun and receives the most energy. Planets farther from the sun receive less heat and have cooler atmospheres. Mercury is much hotter than Neptune, which is very far from the sun. Other factors such as density and pressure also affect the atmospheric temperature.

4 in.
(10 cm)

36 in
(100 cm)

QUICKER

PURPOSE To determine how distance affects a planet's period of revolution.

MATERIALS modeling clay
ruler
yardstick (meter stick)

PROCEDURE

1. Place a walnut-sized ball of clay on one end of the ruler and on one end of the yardstick (meter stick).

2. Hold the yardstick and ruler vertically, side by side, with the edge without the clay ball on the ground.

3. Release both at the same time.

RESULTS The ruler hits the surface first.

WHY? The clay ball on the yardstick has farther to fall than does the ball on the ruler. This is similar to the movement of the planets, which are continuously "falling" around the sun. Mercury, with the shortest distance from the sun, 36 million miles (57.96 million km), takes only 88 Earth days to make its voyage around the sun. Neptune has a much longer path to follow—it is 2,795 million miles (4,498 million km) away from the sun and requires 165 Earth years to complete its period of revolution (time to move around the sun).

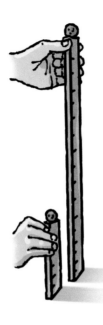

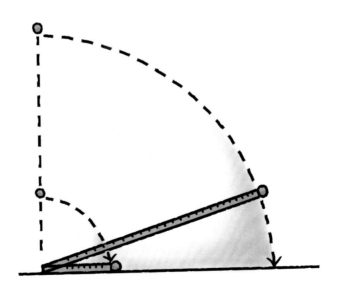

Quicker

BLUE SKY

PURPOSE To determine why Earth is called the blue planet.

MATERIALS drinking glass
flashlight
eyedropper
milk
spoon

PROCEDURE

1. Fill the glass with water.

2. In a darkened room, use the flashlight to direct a light beam through the center of the water.

3. Add 1 drop of milk to the water and stir.

4. Again, shine the light through the water.

RESULTS The light passes through the clear water, but the milky water has a pale blue-gray look.

WHY? The waves of color in white light each have a different size. The particles of milk in the water separate and spread the small blue waves from the light throughout the water, causing the water to appear blue. Nitrogen and oxygen molecules in Earth's atmosphere, like the milk particles, are small enough to separate out the small blue light waves from sunlight. The blue light spreads out through the atmosphere, making the sky look blue from the planet and giving Earth a blue look when it is observed from space. The color in the glass is not a bright blue because more than just the blue light waves are being scattered by large particles in the milk. This happens in the atmosphere when large quantities of dust or water vapor scatter more than just the blue light waves. Clean, dry air produces the deepest blue sky color because the blue waves in the light are scattered the most.

EYE DROPPER

MILK

Back Up

PURPOSE To demonstrate the apparent backward motion of Mars.

MATERIALS helper

PROCEDURE

1. This is an outside activity.

2. Ask a helper to stand next to you and then to start slowly walking forward.

3. Look past your helper's head and notice the background objects that he or she passes.

4. Start walking toward your helper at a faster speed than your helper.

5. Continue to observe the background past your helper's head.

6. Stop and ask your helper to stop when you are about 5 yards (5 m) in front of him or her.

RESULTS At first, you are looking forward to view the background past your helper, but as you take the lead you must look backward to see your helper and the objects beyond.

WHY? Your helper is not going backward; you are simply looking from a different position. Mars was thought by early observers to move forward, stop, go backward, and then go forward again. Actually the planet was continuing forward on its orbit around the sun while Earth was zipping around the sun in one-half the time of Mars' trip. Earth speeds ahead of Mars during part of the time, giving Mars the appearance of moving backward. Mars appears to move forward when Earth races around the orbit and approaches Mars from behind. This apparent change in the direction of Mars is called retrograde motion.

RED SPOT

PURPOSE To demonstrate the movement in Jupiter's red spot.

MATERIALS wide-mouthed jar, 1 gallon (4 liters)
1 tea bag
pencil

PROCEDURE

1. Fill the jar with water.

2. Open the tea bag and pour the tea leaves into the water.

3. Insert the pencil into the center of the water.

4. Move the pencil quickly in a small circle until the tea leaves group and begin to swirl in the center area of the water.

RESULTS The tea leaves group in a spiraling funnel shape.

WHY? The stirring creates a vortex (a mass of liquid or gas that whirls in the jar, forming a cavity in the center toward which things are pulled). The tea leaves are pulled toward the center of the vortex created by the rotating water. The red spot seen on Jupiter is a massive hurricane large enough to swallow three Earths. It is believed that red particles are swirled by moving gases as were the tea leaves, creating the massive storm that has not changed in appearance for as long as people have been able to view Jupiter.

GLIMMER

PURPOSE To determine why Jupiter's rings shine.

MATERIALS flashlight

baby powder in a plastic shaker

PROCEDURE

1. In a darkened room, place the flashlight on the edge of a table.

2. Hold the open powder container below the beam of light.

3. Quickly squeeze the powder container.

RESULTS The beam of light is barely visible before the powder is sprayed into it. After spraying powder into the light beam, the specks of powder glisten, making the light path visible.

WHY? Light is not visible unless it can be reflected to your eye. The tiny specks of powder act like the fine particles in the rings around Jupiter in that they reflect the sun's light. Jupiter's rings are 34,000 miles (54,400 km) from the planet's cloud tops. The material in these rings is thought to come from Io, the innermost of Jupiter's four large moons. Io is the only known moon with active volcanoes, and it is possible that the ash from these volcanoes forms Jupiter's rings.

HIDDEN

PURPOSE To demonstrate how Mercury's position affects the observation of its surface.

MATERIALS desk lamp
ruler
pencil

PROCEDURE

1. Turn the lamp on with the glowing bulb facing you.

CAUTION: Do not look directly into the lamp.

2. Grasp the pencil in the center with the print on the pencil facing you.

3. Hold the pencil at arm's length from your face and about 6 inches (15 cm) from the glowing bulb.

RESULTS The print cannot be read on the pencil, and the color of the pencil is difficult to determine.

WHY? The light behind the pencil is so bright that it is difficult to see the surface of the pencil. In a similar way, the glare of the sun behind the planet Mercury makes it difficult to study the planet's surface. Mercury is less than half the size of Earth and the closest planet to the sun. From Earth, astronomers are looking almost directly into the sun when they view Mercury. The first photographs of one-third of the planet's surface were taken in 1974 and 1975 when the Mariner 10 space probe flew about 200 miles (320 km) from the surface of Mercury.

BIG RED

PURPOSE To produce the material that causes the surface of Mars to have its red color.

MATERIALS 1 paper towel

1 steel wool soap pad

saucer

rubber gloves (like those used to wash dishes)

PROCEDURE

1. Fold the paper towel in half twice and place it in the saucer.

2. Run warm water from the faucet over the steel wool pad to remove as much of the soap as possible.

3. Place the wet steel wool pad in the center of the paper towel in the saucer.

4. Place the saucer where it will not be disturbed for 5 days.

5. Observe the steel wool pad periodically during the 5 days.

6. After 5 days, put on rubber gloves and pick the pad up and rub between your fingers.

RESULTS The pad, which started out as a hard, silvery metal, becomes a reddish powder.

WHY? Steel wool contains the metal iron, which combines with oxygen in the air to form rust (a reddish powder). The soil on Mars is composed mostly of the elements silicon and oxygen mixed with metals including iron and magnesium. An abundance of iron oxide, the combination of iron and oxygen that is called rust, gives Mars its reddish color. Storms in the thin atmosphere of the planet cause winds to swirl the red dust and sand, which form a red cloud that covers the surface of Mars for weeks and months at a time.

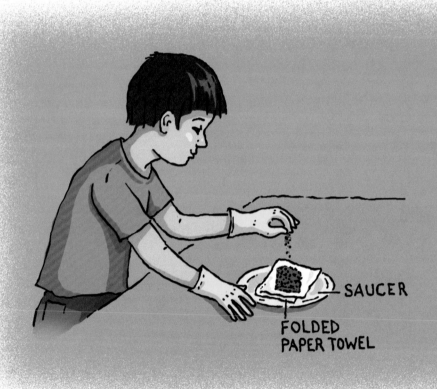

SAUCER

FOLDED
PAPER TOWEL

PEEPER

PURPOSE To determine when the planet Mercury is the most visible from Earth.

MATERIALS cellophane tape
black marking pen
desk lamp
basketball
yardstick (meter stick)

PROCEDURE

1. Center a piece of tape across the opening of a desk lamp. The tape should not touch the light bulb.

2. Use a marking pen to mark a small dot on the tape above the center of the light bulb.

3. Position the lamp so that the bulb faces you.

4. Turn the light on and stand 1 yard (1 m) in front of the bulb.

5. Close your left eye and look at the dot on the tape with your open right eye.

6. Slowly move your body to the left until the dot appears just slightly to the right of the light bulb.

7. Stand in this position while holding a basketball in front of your face. Continue to keep your left eye closed.

8. Move the ball so that it blocks your view of the light bulb but allows you to see the dot on the tape.

More of Janice VanCleave's Wild, Wacky, and Weird Astronomy Experiments

RESULTS The dot is easily seen when it is to the side of the bulb and the basketball blocks out the light from the bulb.

WHY? The planet Mercury can be seen from Earth with your naked eye just before the sun rises in the morning and sets below the horizon in the afternoon. The basketball in this experiment represents the horizon of Earth, the dot is Mercury, and the light bulb is the sun. The position of these materials demonstrates that only when the sun's blinding light is below Earth's horizon can the planet Mercury peep above the horizon and be seen easily.

CURVES

PURPOSE To demonstrate the effect of forces on orbital movement.

MATERIALS

2 chairs
masking tape
yardstick (meter stick)
scissors
string

small paper cup
poster board (dark color)
salt
pencil

PROCEDURE

1. Separate the chairs and tape the ends of the yardstick to the top edge of each chair's back.

2. Cut two 1 yard (1-m) lengths of string.

3. Attach both ends of one string to the yardstick to form a V-shaped support. Secure the ends with tape.

4. Loop the second string over the V-shaped string and use tape to attach the ends to the top rim of the cup, one on each side of the cup. Tie so that the cup is about 4 inches (10 cm) from the floor.

5. Lay the poster board under the hanging cup.

6. Fill the cup with salt.

7. Use the point of a pencil to make a small hole in the bottom of the cup.

8. Pull the cup back and release to allow it to swing forward.

RESULTS The falling salt forms different patterns on the dark paper as the cup swings.

WHY? The cup moves in different patterns because of the forces pulling on the cup. The cup was swung in a back and forth motion, the V-shaped support string pulled it in another direction, and there is the ever-present downward pull of gravity. Planets, like the cup, have different forces acting on them. Each planet spins on its axis and has a forward speed and is pulled on by other planets and its own moon(s), but the big pull is from the sun. The combination of all of these forces guides the planet in the path (orbit) it takes around the sun.

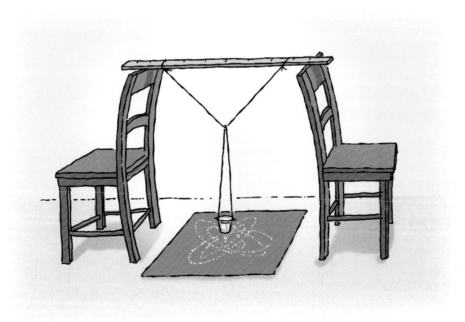

GLOSSARY

BUOYANCY The upward force exerted by a liquid such as water on any object in or on the liquid.

CONCAVE Crescent-shaped.

ESCAPE VELOCITY The speed an object must have to escape Earth's gravitational pull.

GRAVITY A force that pulls toward the center of a celestial body, such as Earth.

GYROSCOPE An instrument with a wheel or disk designed to spin around a central axis; used for aiming and steering ships, planes, or spacecraft.

ORBIT The path of an object around another body; planets moving around the sun.

REVOLUTION The movement around a central point, as Earth moves around the sun.

SATELLITE A small body moving around a larger body.

SPHERE A ball shape.

SPINAL CORD The large bundle of nerves that runs through the discs of the spine.

VELOCITY Speed.

VORTEX The funnel shape of a tornado; a whirling mass of air or water.

WEIGHTLESSNESS A zero pull of gravity.

ZENITH The point in the sky directly above an object, opposite the object's nadir.

FOR MORE INFORMATION

American Astronomical Society (AAS)
   2000 Florida Avenue NW, Suite 300
   Washington, DC 20009-1231
   (202) 328-2010
   Website: http://aas.org
   The AAS is the major organization of professional astronomers in North
   America. Locate an observatory near you, find out about Astronomy
   Ambassadors, and learn about the latest news in astronomy.

National Aeronautics and Space Administration (NASA)
   NASA Headquarters
   300 E. Street SW, Suite 5R30
   Washington, DC 20546
   (202) 358-0001
   Website: http://www.nasa.gov
   NASA is the premier organization for all things space! Join the NASA
   Kids' Club, learn about the International Space Station and historic
   space missions, view solar system photographs, and learn more
   about space technology.

National Science Foundation (NSF)
   4201 Wilson Boulevard
   Arlington, VA 22230
   (703) 292-5111
   Website: http://www.nsf.gov

The NSF is dedicated to science, engineering, and education. Learn how to be a Citizen Scientist, read about the latest scientific discoveries, and find out about the newest innovations in technology.

The Royal Astronomical Society of Canada
203-4920 Dundas Street West
Toronto ON M9A 1B7
Canada
Website: http://rasc.ca
The Royal Astronomical Society of Canada provides many educational resources, including Ask an Astronomer, observation calendars, photographs, and dates of public astronomy events.

Society for Science and the Public
Student Science
1719 N Street NW
Washington, DC 20036
(800) 552-4412
Website: http://student.societyforscience.org
The Society for Science and the Public presents science resources, such as science news for students, the latest updates on the Intel Science Talent Search and the Intel International Science and Engineering Fair, and information about cool jobs and doing science.

WEBSITES

Due to the changing nature of internet links, Rosen Publishing has developed an online list of websites related to the subject of this book. This site is updated regularly. Please use this link to access this list:

http://www.rosenlinks.com/JVCW/astro

FOR FURTHER READING

Ardley, Neil. *101 Great Science Experiments.* New York, NY: DK Ltd., 2014.

Buczynski, Sandy. *Designing a Winning Science Fair Project* (Information Explorer Junior). Ann Arbor, MI: Cherry Lake Publishing, 2014.

Datnow, Claire. *Edwin Hubble: Genius Discoverer of Galaxies* (Genius Scientists and their Genius Ideas). Berkeley Heights, NJ: Enslow Publishers, Inc., 2015.

Gardner, Robert. *A Kid's Book of Experiments with Stars* (Surprising Science Experiments). New York: Enslow Publishing, 2016.

Gifford, Clive. *Astronomy, Astronauts, and Space Exploration* (Watch this Space!). New York, NY: Crabtree Publishing, 2016.

Greve, Tom. *Astronomers* (Scientists in the Field). North Mankato, MN: Rorke Educational Media, 2016.

Henneberg, Susan. *Creating Science Fair Projects with Cool New Digital Tools* (Way Beyond PowerPoint: Making 21st Century Presentations). New York, NY: Rosen Central, 2014.

Kawa, Katie. *Freaky Space Stories* (Freaky True Science). New York, NY: Gareth Stevens Publishing, 2016.

Kuskowski, Alex. *Stargazing* (Out of this World). Minneapolis, MN: Super Sandcastle, 2016.

Levy, Joel. The *Universe Explained* (Guide for Curious Minds). New York, NY: Rosen Publishing, 2014.

McGill, Jordan. *Space Science Fair Projects* (Science Fair Projects). New York, NY: AV2 by Weigl, 2012.

Riggs, Kate. *Moons* (Across the Universe). Mankato, MN: Creative Education/Creative Paperbacks, 2015.

Rockett, Paul. *70 Thousand Million, Million, Million Stars in Space* (The Big Countdown). Chicago, IL: Capstone Raintree, 2016.

Saucier, C. A. P. *Explore the Cosmos Like Neil DeGrasse Tyson: A Space Science Journey.* Amherst, NY: Prometheus Books, 2015.

Spilsbury, Louise. *Space* (Make and Learn). New York, NY: PowerKids Press, 2015.

INDEX

A
artificial gravity, 26–27
atmosphere, 36, 40–41, 50–51
atmospheric temperature, 36–37

E
Earth
    atmosphere of, 40
    blue planet, 40–41
    gravity of, 15, 32, 34
    revolution, 38

F
force, 16–17, 54–55

G
gravity
    artificially produced, 26–27
    effects on height, 30–31
    effect of orbital movement, 54–55
    weightlessness, 28–29
gyroscope, 18–19

I
insulator, 22–23
Io, 46

J
Jupiter
    red spot, 44–45
    rings, 46–47

L
light
    blue light waves, 40–41
    reflections of, 9, 11
liquid in space, 20–21

M
Mariner 10, 48
Mars, 42–43
    atmosphere of, 50–51
    color of, 50–51
    motion of, 42–43
Mercury
    atmosphere of, 36
    distance from the sun, 38
    positional effects, 48–49
    visibility from Earth, 52–53

N
Neptune, 36, 38
Newton's Third Law of Motion, 16

More of Janice VanCleave's Wild, Wacky, and Weird Astronomy Experiments